Recall Everyday

A guide to transform your life…..

Birister Sharma

Dedicated to my loving wife...

Pallabi Devi Sharma

Table of Contents

1. *I am amazing* 1

2. *I can do anything...* 11

3. *I am positive* 21

4. *I celebrate my individuality* 31

5. *I am prepared to succeed* 39

About the author 49

One Word

Do you ever forget to take your breakfast every morning? Do you ever forget to take your lunch every day? Do you ever forget to take your dinner every night? No. Nobody forgets to take his breakfast, lunch and dinner. Nobody can remind us to take our breakfast, lunch and dinner. Because taking breakfast, lunch and dinner are the daily routine of our life. Without it, the mechanisms of our body will not be possible. These are the basic needs of our body.

However, we forget the basic needs of our mind and spirit. The basic needs of our mind and spirit are to motivate ourselves, to inspire ourselves, and to encourage ourselves every day.

The problem with us is that we forget to motivate ourselves every day. We forget to inspire ourselves every day. We forget to encourage ourselves every day. We forget to wake up our inner-strengths and inner-potentials every day. We never feel to motivate, inspire and encourage ourselves every day. We take it for granted.

If you never motivate, inspire and encourage yourself, you'll always find yourself in the web of negativity. You'll trap yourself in the claws of inferiority complex. You'll never discover your true-potentials. You'll lose your self-believe, self-confidence and self-discipline. You'll live in the world of losers. You'll never excel in your entire life.

We all want to change and transform ourselves in our life, but we never try to motivate, inspire and encourage ourselves. We will only change and transform our life when we motivate, inspire and encourage ourselves every day.

You will change and transform your life when you motivate yourself every day.

 You will change and transform your life when you inspire yourself every day.

 You will change and transform your life when you encourage yourself every day.

---***---

1. I am amazing

Nobody can stop you to become amazing in your life, but it is up to you….

Have you ever self-affirmed yourself that you're amazing? If not, then try from today and self-affirm yourself, "I am amazing." You'll really feel not only good but also terrific. And later you'll become the way you self-affirm yourself.

How do you feel when somebody appreciates you for your good deeds or for your good looks or for something related to you? There is no doubt about that you'll not only feel good but also great. It is a human nature that we all love to hear something good about ourselves. There is always a soft corner in our core of hearts to hear something good about ourselves.

It is always remained our burning desire to listen appreciations and compliments from other people whenever or whatever we do something in our life. But what we really forget in our life is to appreciate and compliment ourselves. We start depending on other people's appreciations and compliments even though they may appreciate or compliment us for their own purpose. We start believing in what other people will say or comment on us blindly whether good or bad. We surrender ourselves on the decisions and judgments of other people. Whatever they will decide or judge about us, we follow them unknowingly whether positive or negative. However, we miss our own decisions and judgment. It is very unfortunate that we fail to listen to our own voices, but we listen to other's voices.

If they will say about you, "You're good."

You believe them and feel good whether you're good or not.

If they will say about you, "You're great."

You believe them and feel great whether you're great or not.

If they will say about you, "You're bad."

You believe them and feel bad whether you're bad or not.

Even you see your looks in the mirror, but you wouldn't believe that your looks are good and great until the other people wouldn't appreciate and compliment about your looks. You believe and feel as the other people will say about you. You'll act as their remote-control. Whatever they would say about you, everything resonates in your brain like an auto tune. You start relying on their viewpoints.

But instead of relying on other people's appreciations and compliments, rely on yourself. Appreciate and compliment yourself every day. Don't forget to appreciate and compliment yourself.

Nobody can appreciate and compliment you better than you yourself.

Self-affirm yourself every day, "I am good…..I am great….I am terrific…..I am amazing….. I am successful…." and so on and so forth. Self-affirm yourself until you'll not feel good, great, terrific, amazing and successful. Let your self-affirmation will reach to the layer of your subconscious mind.

Your self-affirmation will act as your magical charm in your life.

It'll change your life.

It'll transform your life.

Before you self-affirm ask yourself, "How do I become good?...."

Then, self-affirm yourself, "I am good."

Think. Dream. Imagine. Visualize. Feel. Act.

Before you self-affirm ask yourself, "How do I become great?...."

Then, self-affirm yourself, "I am great."

Think. Dream. Imagine. Visualize. Feel. Act.

Before you self-affirm ask yourself, "How do I become terrific?...."

Then, self-affirm yourself, "I am terrific."

Think. Dream. Imagine. Visualize. Feel. Act.

Before you self-affirm ask yourself, "How do I feel amazing?...."

Then, self-affirm yourself, "I am amazing."

Think. Dream. Imagine. Visualize. Feel. Act.

Before you self-affirm ask yourself, "How do I become successful?…."

Then, self-affirm yourself, "I am successful."

Think. Dream. Imagine. Visualize. Feel. Act.

There is a great power in your self-affirmation because the way you self-affirm yourself you become in your life.

It is the power of your self-affirmation which will change your believe system in you. And it is your believe system in you which will change your positive attitudes and it is your positive attitudes which will change your actions, and it is your actions which will bring positive results in your life, and it is the positive results which will change your entire life.

If you self-affirm yourself good, you'll become good in your life.

If you self-affirm yourself great, you'll become great in your life.

If you self-affirm yourself successful, you'll become successful in your life.

If you self-affirm yourself failure, you'll become a failure in your life.

You'll only awake and arise your true potentials with your self-affirmation which are hidden from you. Once you start your self-affirmation, you'll discover your dormant treasures which are lying inside you.

But be cautious, never ever self-affirm yourself any negative things about you even by a mistake. Because whatever you self-affirm yourself whether good or bad, whether positive or negative, everything reflects back to you. It is only your self-affirmation which is the key to change your life.

Daily reminders to change your life:

I am amazing…..

I am good….

I am great….

I am terrific….

I am wonderful…

I am incredible…..

I am marvelous….

I am mind-blowing…

I am successful….

I am the best in everything....

---***---

2. *I can do anything...*

With an attitude of 'I Can Do Anything...' you can accomplish anything in your life...

One day a boy went to his guru for consultation. He told his guru that he was the weakest student in his class. He was also very weak in other co-curricular activities in his school. He was good for nothing. He wanted to become good in his studies as well as in other activities in his school. His guru listened to him very keenly.

Then his guru smiled and said candidly, "Don't worry, son!"

"You just say to yourself 'I am good in my studies…..I am good in other activities in my school….' every morning after you wake up from your bed and at night before you go to bed. Do it regularly for three months, and then you come back to me."

The boy jumped with joy.

After three months, the boy went to the guru and gave his heartfelt gratitude for his new transformation.

The guru asked the boy how he could bring changes in his life. Then the boy replied, "Guruji, I did exactly what you've asked me to do."

"I repeat the same thing again and again 'I am good in my studies….I am good in other activities in my school…..' every morning after I wake up, and at night before I go to sleep…."

He continued, "After doing a few days, I realized that only repeating the same thing wouldn't work for me; I have to do something to become really good in my studies as well as in other activities. Then I started concentrating on my lessons harder and harder, and at the same time I started taking part in other activities in my school, and gradually everything improved."

The guru smiled and said, "Well done, son. You can do anything...."

Self-affirm yourself, "I can do anything."

Repeat it more than hundred times in your mind till it reaches to the level of your subconscious mind, and until you'll not feel to do practically in your life.

Then think yourself that you can do anything in your life. Visualize yourself that you can do anything in your life.

How do you feel?

You'll feel confident. You'll start believing in yourself. You'll feel full of energy and enthusiasm. You'll feel positive. You'll feel tremendous willpower within you. You'll feel everything is possible for you. You'll feel everything is at your feet. You'll feel you can achieve everything in your life. You'll feel you can reach anywhere. You'll know what to do in your life. You'll know the real mission of your life.

Your self-affirmation makes you realize your true potentials.

What is the basic difference between a winner and a loser?

A winner always self-affirms himself, "I can do anything……" There is no doubt in his mind. He has clear-cut intentions and goals in his life. He believes in himself. He is a positive thinker. He is a dreamer as well as a doer.

On the other hand, a loser always self-affirms himself, "I can't do anything...." There are hundreds of doubts in his mind. He has no clear-cut intentions and goals. He doubts himself. He is a negative thinker. He is only a dreamer.

Who makes you a winner and a loser?

You make yourself a winner and a loser. Nobody can make you.

You're responsible for your own success and failure.

'I can do anything....' means you're commanding yourself.

Your mind and body starts responding to you to do anything as you self-affirm yourself 'I can do anything....' You'll see possibilities in everything. You'll start leaving your shell of doubts. You'll start believing in your own capabilities.

'I can do anything…' means you believe in yourself fully. You know your true potential. You know what to do and what not to do. You know what is right for you and what is wrong for you. You can make your own decision. You can take your own initiative.

'I can do anything….' means you're capable to do anything. You're eligible to do anything in your life. Your inner jest and enthusiasm will emerge out to do anything on your favour.

'I can do anything…' chant it ritually day in and day out. You'll see a great difference in your life. You'll find new ways and new directions in your life.

'I can do anything….' means you're reminding yourself that nothing is impossible for you. You're unbeatable.

'I can do anything….'means you're prepared to fight back every challenge of your life. You'll become a great challenger. You can challenge everything. You'll become greater than any challenge in your life.

'I can do anything....' means you're dared to fight back every battle of your life. You can defeat every battle of your life. You'll become a daredevil.

'I can do anything..." is the mantra which transforms an ordinary man into an extra-ordinary man.

Mahatma Gandhi was an ordinary man when he began his career as a lawyer in South Africa. However, it was his attitude 'I can do anything.....I can lead my people.....I can liberate my nation from the yoke of foreign power.....' he led his countrymen and fought against the mighty British Empire and liberated his motherland, India. He became the father of the nation when India got her independence.

It is an attitude of 'I can do anything….' that a blind man can do anything in his life. For instance, John Milton, who was blind, but with his 'I can do anything….' attitude wrote the famous poem, 'The Paradise Lost.'

It is an attitude of 'I can do anything….' that Helen Killer despite her blindness she became the famous author. She wrote many novels in English Literature.

It is an attitude of 'I can do anything….' that Madam Curie and Pirie Curie, in spite of the uncountable hurdles in their lives, they had invented radium.

It is an attitude of 'I can do anything….' that Tenzing Norgay who had conquered the great summit of Mount Everest in 1953.

It is an attitude of 'I can do anything…' that Chanakya who was a poor Brahmin and destitute, but with his 'I can do anything....' attitude he had overthrown the mighty Nanda Dynasty with the help of his disciple, Chandragupta Maurya, and established Mauryan Dynasty.

It is an attitude of 'I can do anything.....' that Alexander dared to conquer the entire world at the age of 21.

It is an attitude of 'I can do anything.....' that Columbus had sailed his ship in order to discover the new lands, and discovered America.

With the attitude of 'I can do anything...' you can do anything in your life. You can achieve anything in your life. You can reach anywhere in your life. You can touch any height in your life. Nothing is impossible for you. You'll become a winner and conqueror in your life.

'I can do anything....' is the most powerful self-affirmation to affirm yourself every day. It'll act as your magic potion. It'll drive you throughout your life in every situation, both good times and bad times.

Daily reminders to change your life:

I can do anything in my life….

I can work anything in my life…

I can handle every situation of my life….

I can fight back every challenge of my life….

I can change my life…

I can transform my world….

---***---

3. I am positive

It is only your positive mindset which will hold you tight in every harsh thunderstorm of your life....

When you say yourself, "I am positive" it means you're injecting a positive energy within you. You'll feel positive in everything around you. You'll feel like you're reborn in this world. You'll feel the positive currents flowing inside you.

Your mind, body and soul are interconnected with each other. The way you feel in your mind in the same way you'll feel in your body and in your soul. If your mind feels positive energy, then both your body and soul will automatically feel the same positive energy.

Positive in and positive out. Negative in and negative out.

If you develop a positive mindset in your life, then you'll always see the positive outcome in your life. On the other hand, if you develop a negative mindset in your life, you'll always see a negative outcome in your life. It is like as you sow as you reap.

Why many people couldn't do well in their lives despite they have their skills and talents? The only reason behind is that they have negative mindsets. They see negative things in everything. Their mindsets are engrossed in the whirlpools of confusions and doubts and ifs and buts, and as a result, they can't take any initiative in their lives. And in the end they start blaming games and give their silly excuses.

What is the success formula of your life? Have you ever asked yourself?

No.

The only success formula of your life is to stay positive in every situation of your life no matter whatsoever happens to you.

If you stay positive in your bad times, you'll enjoy your life when the good times return in your life.

What will do when you're stuck in the midst of furious thunderstorms on your way back to home?

You'll have to wait till the thunderstorms will stop, and everything will become normal. You'll never fight back against the furious thunderstorms. In the same fashion, you'll never fight back against the bad times. You can only hold yourself tight with cool and calm.

Bad times and good times are like pass and parcel; they are the parts of your life. They are like seasons. You never stop them. You'll have to face your bad times in order to witness your good times. You'll only witness your good times when you'll face your bad times with positive mindsets and positive attitudes.

There are many people who try to run away from their bad times. But, they never succeed. They can't run away from their bad times.

It is your bad times that test how much caliber you have and how much you have a positive mindset and positive attitude within you. The only way to tackle your bad times and harsh situations of your life is to remain positive.

The successful people are those who have seen and faced a thousand times bad times in their lives. They have never run away from their bad times, but they have faced all the bad times with their positive mindsets and positive attitudes.

Why it is usually seen that a patient recovers fifty percent from his illness before the doctor prescribes him any medicine?

It is because a patient has a positive believe that as the doctor examines him, he will be alright. There is such a great affect in positive thoughts and positive beliefs.

It is your positive thoughts and positive beliefs that will change and transform your life.

What is the difference between a positive man and a negative man?

A positive man always sees opportunity in every calamity.

But a negative man always sees calamity in every opportunity.

When a positive man talk, he will talk about success. He will talk about opportunities. He will talk about chances. He will talk about possibilities. He will talk about his strengths. He will talk about solutions. He will talk about new things. He will talk about new ideas and plans. He will talk about hope and aspiration. He will talk about achievements.

On the contrary, a negative man talks completely different. He will talk about failure. He will talk about misfortunes. He will talk about the difficulties. He will talk about problems. He will talk about his past mistakes. He will talk about his weaknesses. He will give his excuses. He will only talk about negative things.

Be aware of negative people. Never ever surround yourself in the midst of negative people. Because negative people always speak negative things to you, they will corrupt your mind, body and soul with their negative talks, negative ideas, negative plans, negative decisions, and negative actions. They are like the weeds in the fertile land of your life.

Always surround yourself in the midst of positive people. They will help you. They will guide you. They will flourish your life with their positive talks, positive ideas, positive plans, positive decisions, and positive actions.

Positive says: I am good.

Negative says: I am bad.

Positive says: Life is beautiful.

Negative says: Life is ugly.

Positive says: I am strong.

Negative says: I am weak.

Positive says: I am capable to do anything.

Negative says: I am not capable to do anything.

Positive says: I am confident.

Negative says: I am not confident.

Positive says: I am bold.

Negative says: I am not bold.

Positive says: I am happy.

Negative says: I am unhappy.

Positive says: I am peaceful.

Negative says: I am disturbed.

Positive says: I am successful.

Negative says: I am unsuccessful.

For a positive man every day is a new day to begin something new.

Daily reminders to change your life:

I am positive.....

I am good in everything.....

I am confident in myself.....

I am happy with myself.........

I am content with myself......

I am peaceful......

I am great.......

I am independent.....

---***---

4. I celebrate my individuality

Life is short and beautiful…. Don't forget to celebrate your life…

You're unique. You're different. Don't compare yourself with anyone. What you can do the other people can't do. You've different qualities. You've different skills and talents. You're a blessed one. Love your uniqueness. Enjoy your uniqueness. Celebrate your uniqueness. Love your own skills and talents. Enjoy your skills and talents.

Don't forget what you have in your life. Utilize whatever you've for your own growth and development. Uplift your own life. Make your own life. Build your own life. Don't waste your time. Don't waste your life.

Don't search your happiness in the outside world. Search it inside you. Nobody can make you happy. Only you can make yourself happy. Enjoy your happiness. Celebrate your happiness. Share your happiness with your beloved ones. It'll double your happiness.

Don't search the treasure house in the external world. Search it in your internal world. If you're determined in your chosen goal, you'll get it. Nobody can stop you.

Discover yourself what you really want to do in your life. Discover your own strength and weakness. Discover your potential and caliber. And give your best. Give your hundred percent efforts whatever you do in your life.

Don't wander in search of unwanted desires in your life. Control your emotions and wild desires and direct it to the right direction. Find out your true purpose of your life. Find out the true meaning of your life.

Be the pathfinder of your own life. Set your own aims and objectives of life. Without aims and objectives in your life, you'll always wander like a nomad, living an unsettled life.

A man without aims and objectives is like a bird without wings.

Work for your own progress. Work for your own growth and development. Work for your own greatness. Work for your own dignity. Work for your own excellence. Think practical and live practical.

You can make what you want to make in your life. You can build what you want to build in your life. You can create what you want to create in your life. You're the maker of your own life. You're the builder of your own life. You're the creator of your own life.

Free yourself from your self-doubts. Your self-doubts are the murderers of your skills and talents. Free yourself from your worries and anxieties. They are the thieves of your happiness and peace. Free yourself from your bad habits. They are the virus of your good qualities. Free yourself from your weaknesses. They are the enemies of your infinite strengths. Free yourself from your egos. They are the killers of your beautiful life.

Accept the challenges of your life. Face them with your brave heart. But don't try to escape from them. The more you try to escape from them, the more they chase you. You can only counter them when you face them. Never afraid of the challenges of your life. The challenges of life are the parts of your life. Life means challenge.

Every challenge brings you new opportunity in your life.

It is up to you what you want to love and what's not to love. It is up to you what you want to like and what not to like. It is up to you what you want to choose and what not to choose. It is up to you what you want to enjoy in your life and what's not to enjoy in your life. It is up to you what you want to celebrate in your life and what not to celebrate in your life. It is up to you what you want to do in your life and what not to do in your life. Everything depends upon you. Nobody can force you to do anything. You're the ruler of your own world. You're the king of your own kingdom.

Live your life in such a manner that every day is your festive season.

Live your life in such a manner that today is your glorious day.

Live your life in such a manner that today is your last day.

Live your life in such a manner that you have no regrets in your life.

Live your life in such a manner that everybody remembers you.

Daily reminders to change your life:

I love myself….

I love my life…

I love my world…

I love my family…

I enjoy myself…

I enjoy my life....

I enjoy my world....

I celebrate the beauty of my life....

I celebrate the treasure of my world....

I celebrate my individuality....

---***---

5. I am prepared to succeed

A prepared man never loses anything in his life....

In the year 1191 A.D the first battle of Tarain was fought between Prithviraj Chauhan of Ajmer, the Hindu king and Muhammad Gori, Muslim invader of Ghur from Afghanistan. The battle was furious and fatal. In that battle the forces of Prithviraj Chauhan were fully prepared from all around, therefore they fought bravely and defeated the mighty forces of Muhammad Gori. And in the end Muhammad Gori was captured along with his remaining soldiers. He was brought in chain like an ordinary soldier, parading in the streets of Ajmer and placed before Prithviraj Chauhan. The ministers and advisers of Prithviraj Chauhan advised him to punish Muhammad Gori. However, Prithviraj Chauhan released him, and asked him not to dare to invade again in his land.

Muhammad Gori felt humiliated, and returned in his land in Afghanistan. He vowed to himself that he wouldn't take rest and sleep until he wouldn't take his revenge. He didn't allow his wound to heal. He prepared himself day and night. He rebuilt the strong foundation of his commanders and soldiers and prepared them fully like iron and steel for the next battle against Prithiviraj Chauhan for one year completely.

On the other hand, Prithviraj Chauhan and his commanders and soldiers spent their time in merry making and in luxuries. They considered that

Muhammad Gori and his soldiers wouldn't dare to attack them again after the fatal defeat at their hands. Therefore, they stopped their preparations and spent their entire time in drinking wine and gambling. But their assumptions were utterly wrong.

As per plan Muhammad Gori attacked on Prithviraj Chauhan second time in 1192. The soldiers of Prithviraj Chauhan were unprepared; they had no clue how the soldiers of Muhammad Gori surrounded and attacked them. They were terribly defeated by the soldiers of Muhammad Gori. In that decisive battle, Prithviraj Chauhan was killed. And the entire kingdom of Ajmer was captured by Muhammad Gori.

Your life is like a battle. You're like a soldier. You never know who will attack you, when and how. You never know who your friend is; and who your enemy is.

Your friend doesn't only mean anybody, but it may be you yourself. Your enemy doesn't only mean anybody, but it may be you yourself.

Bhagwat Gita says, ***"A man's own self is his friend. A man's own self is his foe."***

Your enemy resides both internally and externally. You've to keep your vigilant eyes day and night. You've to guard yourself. You've to observe and analyze yourself every day and every night. You've to figure out your strong points and weak points. Because your strong points will build your life; and your weak points will wreck your life. You've to discover your good habits and bad habits. Your good habits will enrich your life; and your bad habits will ruin your life.

You've to figure out your positive attitudes and negative attitudes. Your positive attitudes will upgrade your life; and your negative attitudes will degrade your life. You've to check and recheck yourself every day. You've to prepare yourself every second, every minute, every hour, every day, every week, every month and every year. You've to prepare yourself both mentally and physically.

Your success and failure both are on your hands. You're responsible for your own success and failure. If you want to glimpse the glorious moment of your success, then you've to prepare yourself. Without preparation, you can't achieve anything in your life.

Your preparation is the only source of your success and glory. Nobody in this entire world will succeed without preparation. The moment you'll stop your preparation in your life, the very moment the countdown of your failure and downfall will start. And the moment you'll start your preparation in your life, the very moment the countdown of your success and glory will start.

Many successful people witness failure and downfall later in their life. Why?

The only reason behind their failure and downfall is because they stop their continuous preparations. They have forgotten that nothing remains permanent. Neither success nor failure is permanent. You'll only retain and maintain your success and glory with your continuous preparation.

Your success always demands continuous preparation from you. Are you ready to prepare yourself? Ask yourself every moment and every day.

Prepare yourself before you execute anything in your life, you'll get enough time to think; you'll get enough time to plan; you'll get enough time to analyze;

you'll get enough time to research yourself; you'll get enough time to know your potentials; you'll get enough time to make your decisions. You'll never witness your failure and downfall in your life if you prepare yourself every moment and every day.

Nobody can defeat a prepared mind.

Your preparation will lead you to the door of your success and glory.

Daily reminders to change your life:

I am prepared to succeed….

I am prepared to win…

I am prepared to challenge…

I am prepared to march ahead…

I am prepared to lead myself…..

I am prepared to control myself….

I am prepared to become a self-reliant…

I am prepared to live a glorious life….

---***---

5 *Daily Reminders To Change Your Life!*

1. I am amazing......

2. I can do anything......

3. I am positive......

4. I celebrate my individuality.....

5. I am prepared to succeed......

About the author

Birister Sharma is a full time author. He is also an avid reader. He loves reading, writing, and motivation. He has penned down dozens of self-help motivational books and novels so far.

You may contact him @ birister2007@gmail.com